Affirmations for a Young King

Written by Aisha

Designed by Valeria Leonova

Dear Young King,

Today, you may be a little King, but even now,

your power is greater than you know. Do not dim

your light for this world...we need you!

Love you,

-Aisha

I am unstoppable

I AM FOCUSED

I AM BEAUTIFUL INSIDE AND OUT

I matter

My feelings matter

I am loved, and I

deserve to be loved

I deserve to be protected

I was born to be a KING,

and I behave as such

I EXPRESS MY FEELINGS...

EVEN WHEN IT'S DIFFICULT

I am fearless

I am mentally, financially,

spiritually and physically

healthy

I AM ACTIVELY WORKING

TOWARD MY GOALS

I am a thoughtful and helpful son,

brother and friend

I am a
BOSS

I am secure in who I am and excited about who I am becoming

I have billion-dollar ideas

I am more than a dreamer;

I am a DO-ER

*I build up
my community*

The world is a better place

because I am in it

I was created to do things

that   have   never   been

done before

I learn something new everyday

I am appreciated by those around me, and I am appreciative of everyone I encounter

I have more than enough

for every situation

I am resourceful

I love my growing body

I stand up for what is right

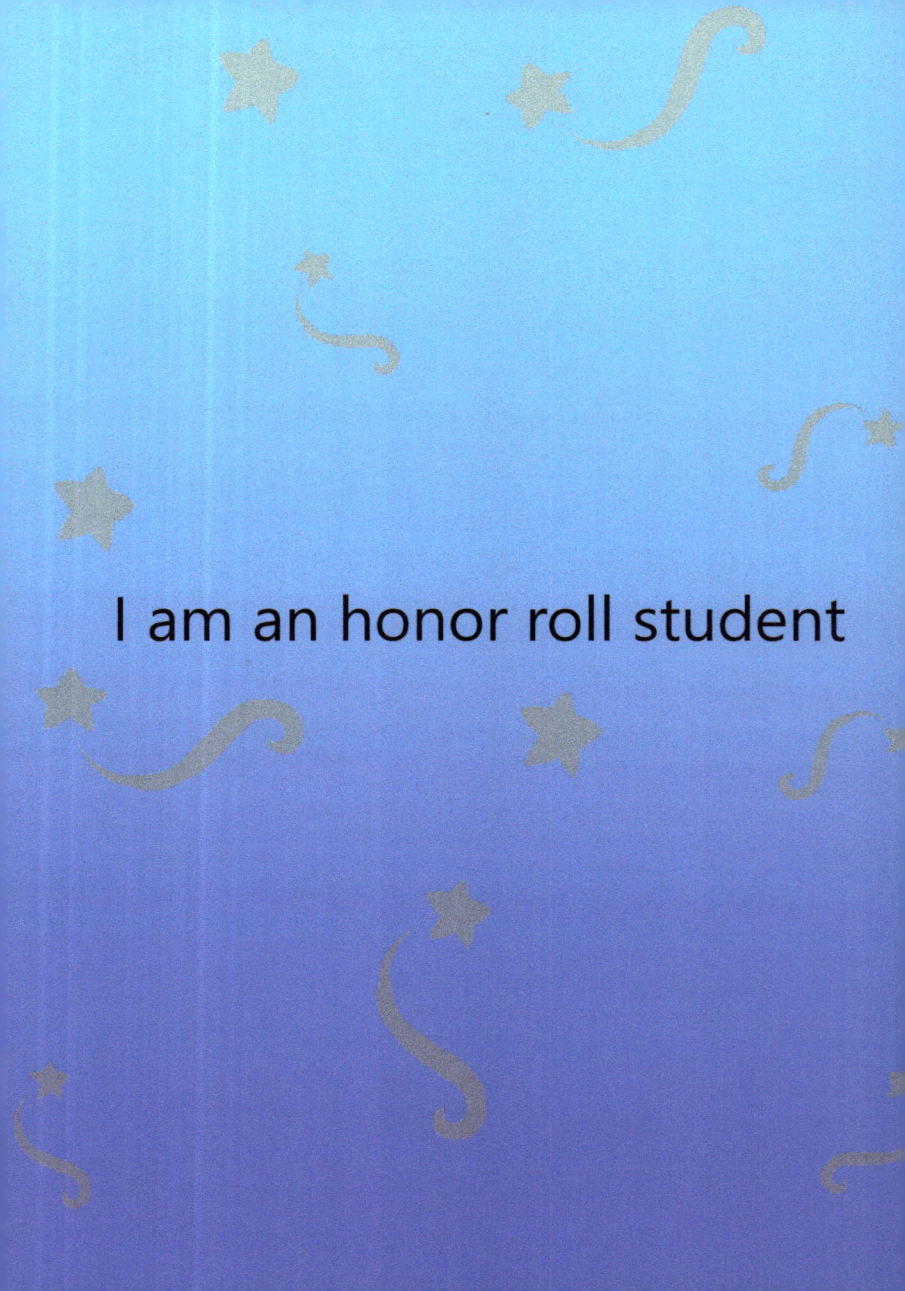

I am an honor roll student

I AM A ROLE MODEL/MENTOR AND I AM SURROUNDED BY MEN THAT FORCE ME TO BE BETTER

My friends are a good influence on me, and I am a good influence on them

I am responsible

I AM ADVENTUROUS

I am a good leader

I am a good listener

I make wise decisions

I attract positivity

I have high expectations

of myself and those

around me

I bring something special

to every space I occupy

I learn from my mistakes

I AM HAPPY

I am ok asking for help when I need it

I was created to beat the odds and challenge negative stereotypes

I expect new opportunities

daily

I am not weird;
I was born to stand
out

I maintain good habits

Everything I start...

I complete

I am proactive

I live a rich lifestyle...

rich in love, happiness,

health and wealth

I am a team player

I am well rounded

I go after what I want

I am well-behaved

I take good care of my body and put thought into my appearance

I understand that it is ok to be

vulnerable

There are scholarships, grants, checks and awards with my name on them

I am not too young to make

my dreams come true

I am powerful, and
that power cannot
be taken away

I celebrate my wins
and the wins of those
around me

TODAY, I AM BETTER
THAN I WAS YESTERDAY

I am free of stress, anxiety and depression

I am a prize!

I AM LIMITLESS WITH

ENDLESS TALENTS

I boldly conquer
the challenges
that come my way

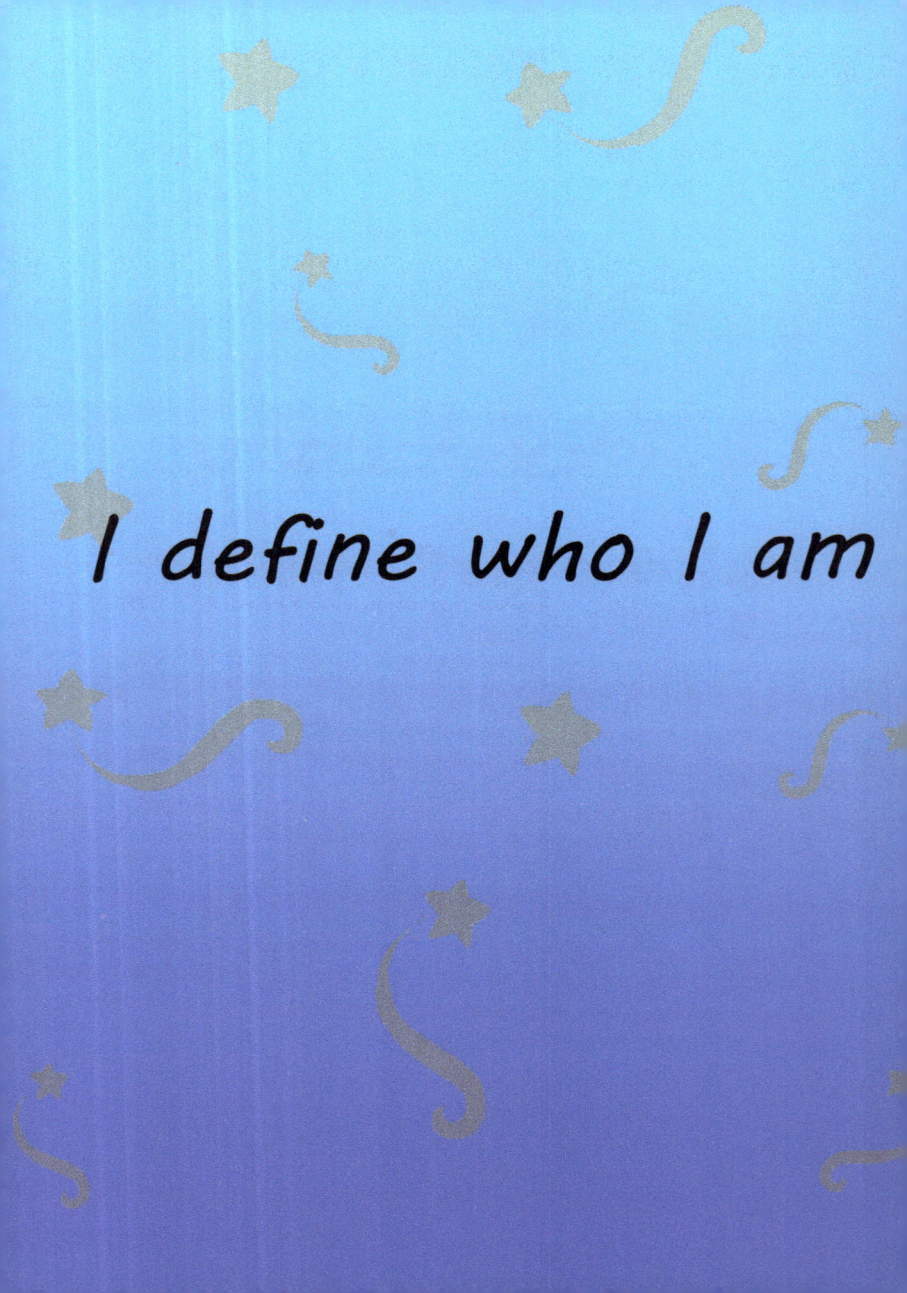

I define who I am

I have an amazing family
and loyal friends that care
about me

I am a magnet
for positive
experiences

I am ENOUGH...
I always have been...
I always will be

This book belongs to _____

www.ingramcontent.com/pod-product-compliance
Lightning Source LLC
Chambersburg PA
CBHW051603010526
44118CB00023B/2801